You Are the Only One For Me

Dani Ann Raven Honeycutt

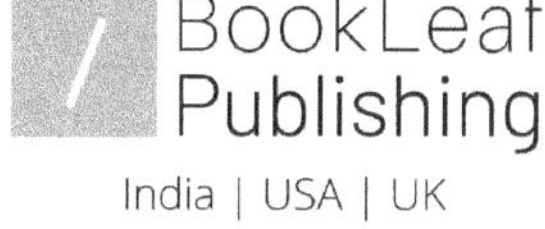

India | USA | UK

Presentation by *BookLeaf Publishing*

Web: www.bookleafpub.com

E-mail: info@bookleafpub.com

ISBN: 9789357211352

First edition 2022

DEDICATION

Time isn't meant to heal all wounds, M'Dear.
Truly seek and ye shall find. Until we meet,
again...Olive Juice.

PREFACE

Come along, I have stories to tell.

Melting Snow

Wrap a blanket tight around,
Stir the logs in my fireplace.
The crackling hiss of cinders and sap
Give a warm glow to my face.

Cup of Cocoa in my hand
A book sits open on my knee
Look out my curtains left agape
To the winter landscape before me

I wait for this time, almost all year
No footprints, no birds, no traffic will pass
I know next comes Melting Snow
So I cherish the moment, for it never lasts.

As seasons change, life reawakens
In higher temps I'm a busy bee
I take a deep breath, and enjoy the sight
For all this will soon be but a memory

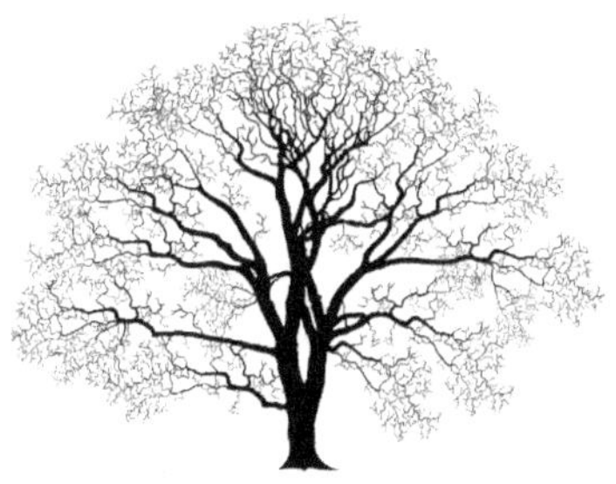

Kneesnhips

They say the eyes are first to go,
Or maybe it's the mind.
As long as I can still dance in the kitchen,
I think I'll be just fine.

Too many people worry of wrinkles,
Or they dye their natural greys.
Even when I can't sing along,
Don't let me lose my sway.

Jump from one foot
Then the other
Make a quick turn
And shake all over

Feel the rhythm rocking through my soul,
Tap my foot and rattle the bones.
Lord, just don't let lose my
Kneesnhips & toes.

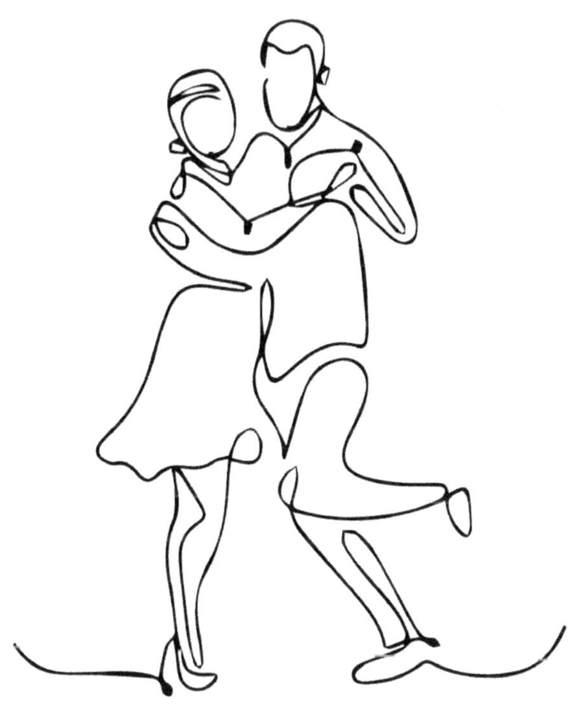

Just Like Magic

Chop and Sautee
Eyeball all the rest
Add a pinch here
And stir the pot

Music up LOUD
Pan on to simmer
Roll out some dough
Steam up the rice

Clean as you cook
Dance to and fro
Flash the heat
Then bring to slow boil

Takes all day
But'cha eat good
Gumbo Night
Just Like Magic for your soul

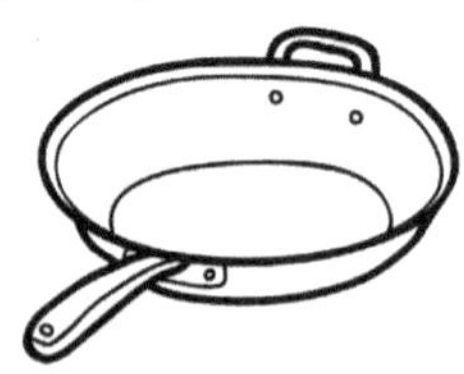

Wild For Wycliff

Getting harder to come by
those well read.
At night play games,
or scroll phones instead.

Give me a book,
whose pages are worn.
Creases and tatters
with spines that are torn.

As I drift away
and see in my dreams:
A Sancho, A Lenny
A Caged Bird that Sings.

Pundits and sayers,
of both sooth and of truth
Are found by my bedside
my own fountain of youth.

The Greeks, and Jung
A few Romans, and Gauls
Nietzsche, Confucius,
Bukowski, and Marx

Some are just tales,
of a life worth living.
Others are filled with
love that's forgiving.

All of them dears
and so close to my heart.
With them my dreams
become works of art.

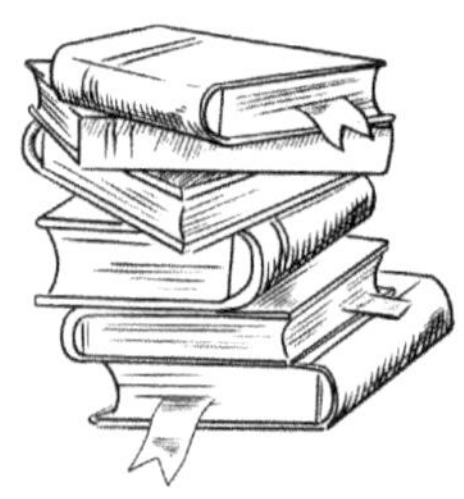

Curbs And Cones

Life is full of Curbs and Cones.
Some roads well traveled,
And others less known.

All of us travel a speedway called life.
A few fully equipped,
Several just there for the ride.

Flashers will indicate speed bumps ahead.
Alleyways darkened,
Can fill you with dread

Smattering of breakdowns, side of the road.
Awaiting the kindness of others,
To get where foretold.

All of us going to some unknown place.
Destined for elsewhere,
Just moving through space

Byways and highways to get us there fast.
Most just concerned,
How to outrun their past

Curbs and Cones will guide us the way.
If you follow the signs,
On life's neverending causeway.

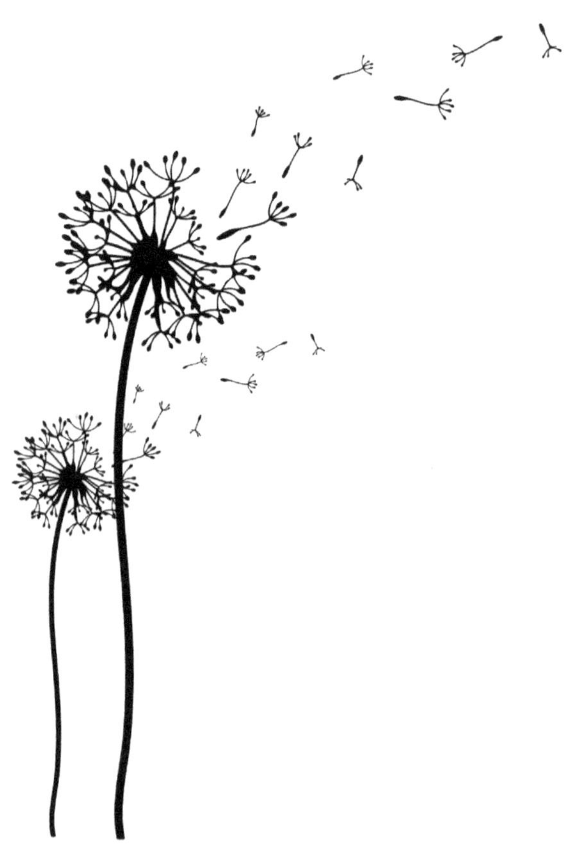

Kiss Me On Oconee

Take me somewhere
    the winter and summer meet
      a land with snow and beaches
    Kiss Me On Oconee

A quiet place,
    we can both sit
      beside ourselves
    with our troubles are far away

Let the time fly by
    as the river flows
      the pines provide shade
    and a place to hide

A warm breeze
    can tousle our hair
      carry the scent of jasmine
    and keep us warm

The songs of birds
    the slap of gators
      and croak of frogs
    the only sounds heard

A secret place
    where our lips can meet
        and no others can intercede
    time alone is time enough

So close I can feel you breathe
    no more of the chase
Won't you please,
    Kiss Me On Oconee?

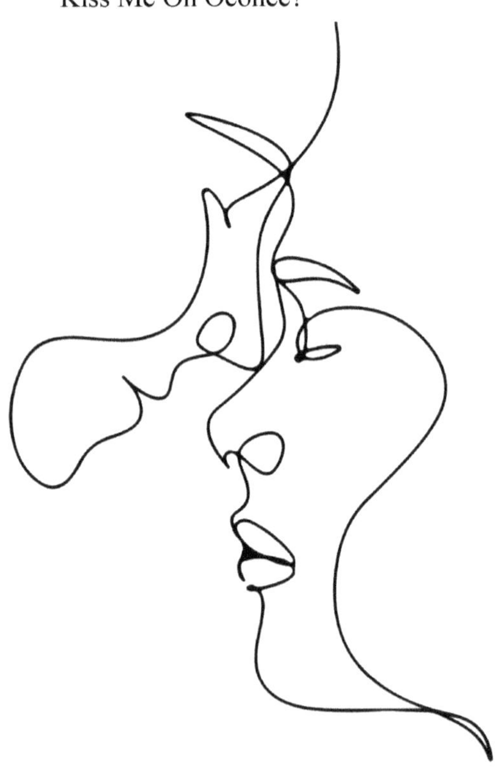

Brisbane Road

Came to see the Cup
How'd my map turn right side up?
Should have brought the board

Now horses running
Instead to the beach sunning
Vacay now restored

Shake it off and grin
Mighty fun mess, once again
Waves won't be ignored

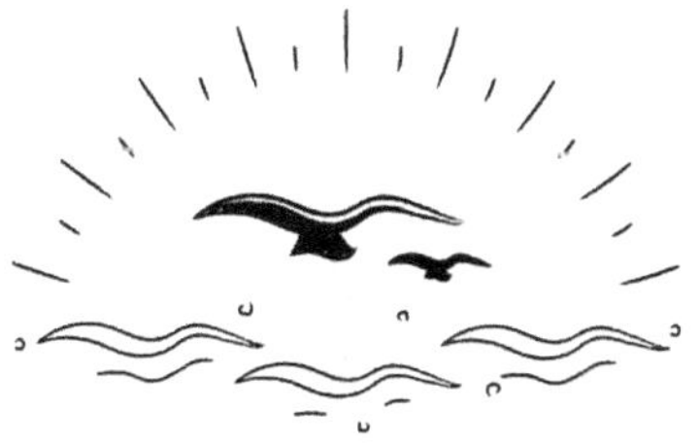

Tiwanaku

As before, I live with purpose
(Hidden just beyond the surface)
Now more familiar with who i am
(And less concerned with where I land)

I hold my head so high and strong
(No worries of where I may belong)
I've made my place within this world
(No longer a browbeat little girl)

I shivagit not the thoughts of others
(Made it through life's perilous blunders)
I've seen the world through other eyes
(Could not count the tears I've cried)

I've lost and won a million battles
(Gone hell for leather in my travels)
Made it through them all alright
(I've taught my heart how to take flight)

I find the joy in simple pleasures
(Am not worried for worldly treasures)
Found a path that's mine uniquely
(Learned to know myself quite dearly)

Have not the time for listless doubts
(Begin a task, I see throughout)
I know now we make our own place
(Within this cosmic living space)

Mine is filled with joy and passion
(I had to learn to make that happen)
No longer fear what I'll never know
(Or concern myself with how far to go)

See me one day, the next I'm gone
(Bearing down on Babylon)
No real answers, just ideals
(No more long-winded pessimistic spiels)

Used to worry I'd fade as the Tiwanaku
(Realize now that was more about you)
I've lived on, so proud and free
(I sometimes wish you had just joined me)

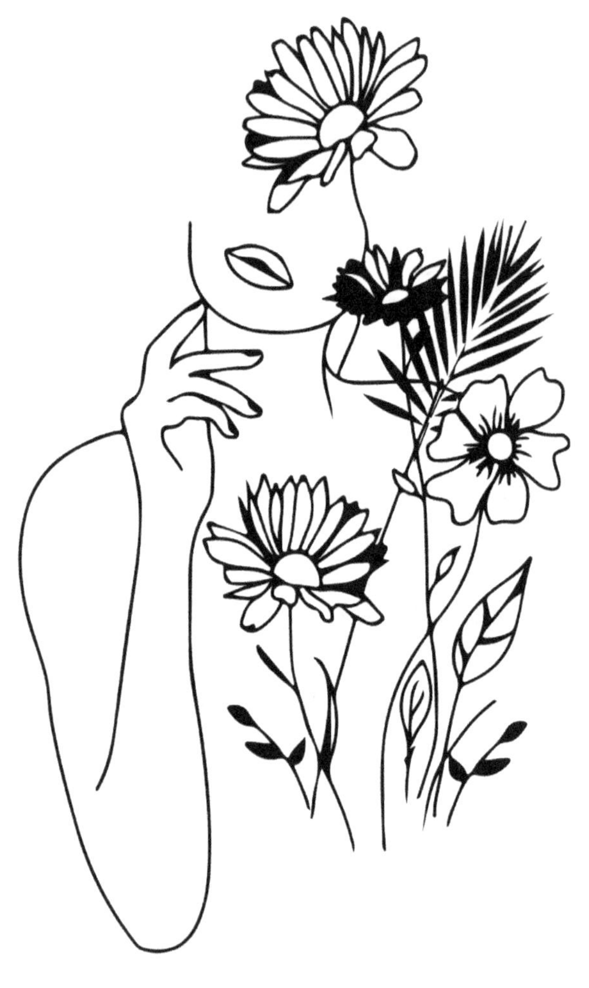

Take The Backroads

I Take the Backroads
To make More Memories.
I carry them
While my heart is a sea

Watch the dawn from a Badlands bluff
See the fields all filled with rust
Made the choice to live organic
Wonder where tf my past went

Seen the sunset from both coasts
Sauntered in, and dipped my toes
Looking for the life Fantastic
Barely take the time to unpack

Wander here, and wonder there
Found myself near Blackbeard's lair
Saw the folks that never roamed
Still have yet to find my home

Collect t-shirts and bric-a-brac
Watch the ponies run round The Track
Wax and wane philosophic
Wish I knew where my all my time was

Load up on snacks down south at Pops
Hopped a train, then caught a bus
Made it north where nights are clear
Beneath the stars, Universe's mirror

Caught some shows, and heard some tunes
Wrote down even more platitudes
What's that view like from afar?
Top is down, I'm back in my car

I Take the Backroads
To make More Memories
I cherish them
Alone, when I can't sleep

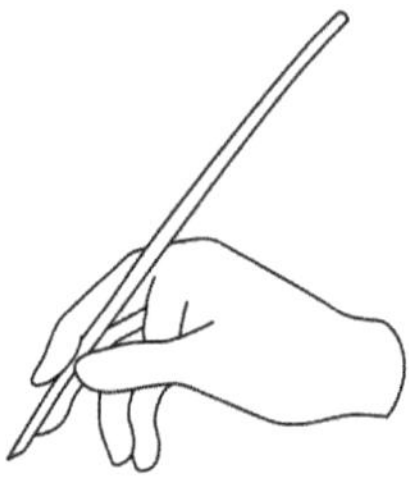

Thunderheart

Mane black and tousled
Smells sweet as the hay he rolls in
Brown eyes that feel like home
My safety is found here

Has grace that knows no bounds
A well worn soul within
Though only four by age
Kindness as no other holds

Content with the simplest of gestures
Peppermints and a pat
A tickle from his nuzzle and a chuff
Are my greatest rewards

Never knowing what the next day holds
Through calms and storms
Life only granted one guarantee
With him I can take on the world

His steady staccato thump
Matches the beat of my heart
Only quicker in pace
This is the feeling of freedom

There is no distance too great
Nor speed too swift
To withstand the hooves
Of my Thunderheart

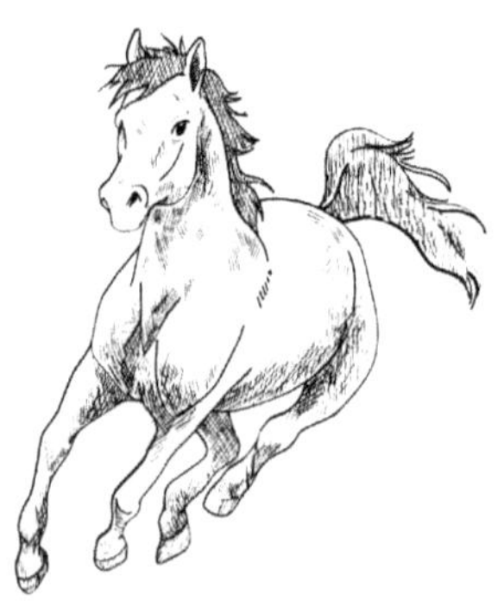

Owen's Leap

soaring, free falling
     waves lap, and carefree gasps all around
      submerge and let my heart beat
       in time to the random thumps
    and thuds above
     sound travels different underwater

     kick and reach after touch down;
     avoid collision
      tuck the knees just before the.
  surface breaks
a rolled ankle, or scraped elbow
    is tended to on shore

    rope swing is in full action
      as others gather in a line for their turn
     tossing it back to shore as each safely
  lands
two knots so everyone is big enough
     well timed high fives from rock to Rope

    feeling tethered
     then   loose
      and   free
as I let go and make the leap

from ground to flight and
then submerging
breaking through the surface tension

afterwards floating
sunlight filters through the leaves
touches my face
and arms and legs
leaving me browner than when I came

the scratchiness of a well used towel
sun bleached and beckoning warmth
smells linger of creek water,
cookouts and linen
dogs are awaiting dropped treasures

weariness abates
fulfillment from a day wellspent
for now all is as it should be
right within the world and myself

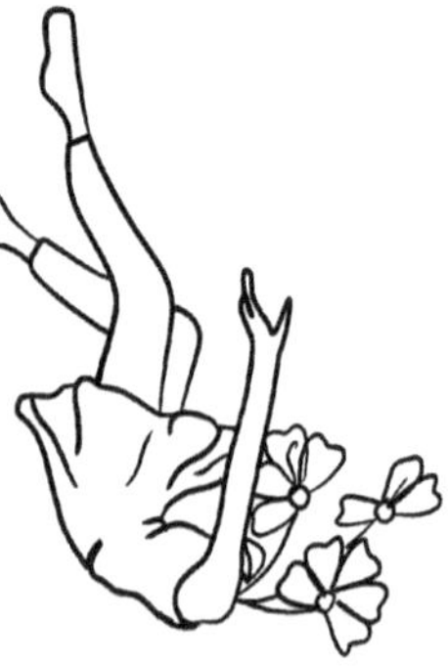

Isolate

Made it to L.A. once
Saw bars, cars, electric guitars
Didn't dip my toes in the sand
Managed to see a marching band

Made it to South Dakota
Came close enough to touch a buffalo
Slept out beneath the stars
Collected dust in my jars

Made it to Michigan
Saw the sand covered in snow
Met a Dowagiac Chief
Though that meeting was brief

Made it to New York
Traffic didn't bother me much
Lucked into a play
On the world famous Broadway

Made it to most the places
I said I'd go
That Thailand trip
Still needs funds to equip

Made it to Happy,
Smile rarely fades
Funny how life works
To Isolate was one of the perks

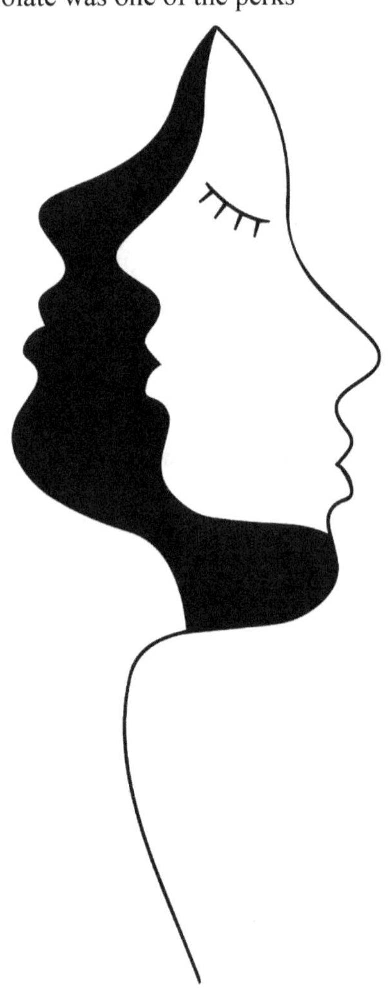

Higher Standard

Jump both feet, into each occasion
Led by gut, with no dissuasion
No such thing as coincidence
Love your life in present tense
No direction, no worries
No fear, all glory
Guided by a higher hand
Grounded by a head of sand
Leading to a greater calling
Nonesuch of a fear of falling
I get there, when I get there's good
Just flow through life as a river would

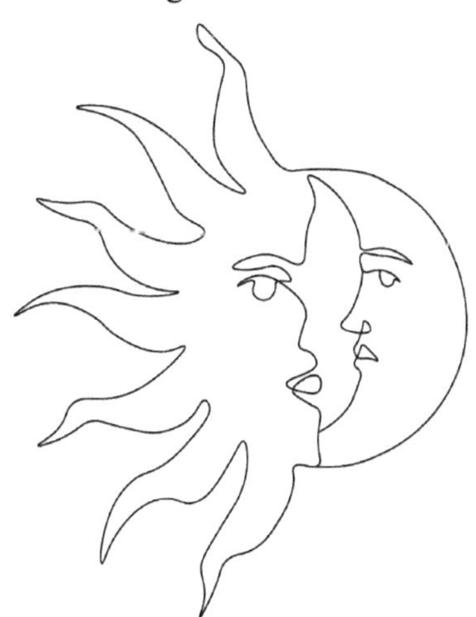

Curly Jack (and the) Malibu SS

Curly Jack took a load up north,
Wasn't definite on the course.
Took some byways, the scenic route.
Ended up at the Delta's Mouth.

Decided not to take the load back home.
Tasked a friend, said he would owe 'em.
Found a fille, they danced all night.
Felt the start of his new life.

Pretty as a picture, just as sweet.
When morning came, she ordered tea.
Out and about bumped into her man.
Two black eyes, sight not quite the same.

Curly Jack never one to sulk,
Went back out, he wasn't broke.
Grabbed a wine cake, heard some jazz.
Got turned around on Tchoupitoulas.

Wandered down and through St. Charles.
Amazed by the beauty of their yards.
Some grew flowers, some grew moss,
There was no place that trash was tossed.

Seen a madame out on a stroll.
She seemed too high class for him, though.
Found a cher, selling voodoo trinkets.
Took the chance, gave a sultry wink.

Three weeks later, he's done her wrong.
Got no choice but to mosey at dawn.
Sees a Ferry Boat from Dauphine.
Heads that way never losing steam.

Tossed his brindle, jumped on time.
Took a glance and read her sign.
Curly Jack had caught the Malibu SS.
Maybe this time I'll just head west.

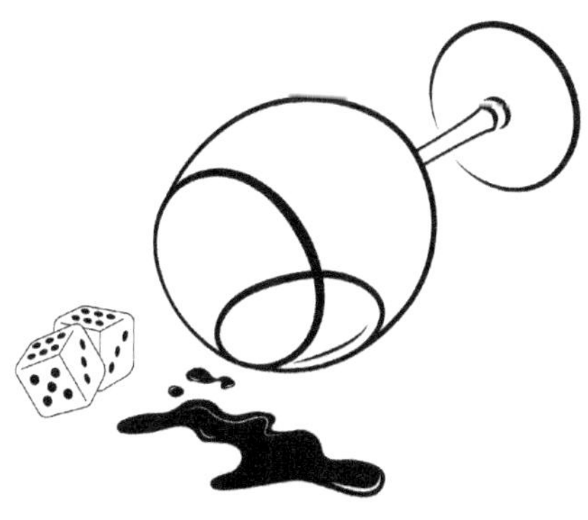

Out Of Alcatraz

Comin' to you straight Out of Alcatraz
The beats, the strums, with all that Razzmatazz
Show the kids how to do the bump
Lay me down some crazy funk

Met a sista, she was a soldier.
Taught me what my heart was good for
Had some lessons hard to learn
Can't stop the fire, for which I burn

Told a tale, wide and far
Some fell from a way off star
Lost the path, went way off course
She's out there lonely on her horse

Some of us go round and round
Others are just bound for sound
Teach a songbird melody
Taught a jailbird what is free

All my life just wanted more
A Hallucinogenic Toreador
Out here bound by no restraints
Free life baby, ain't got complaints

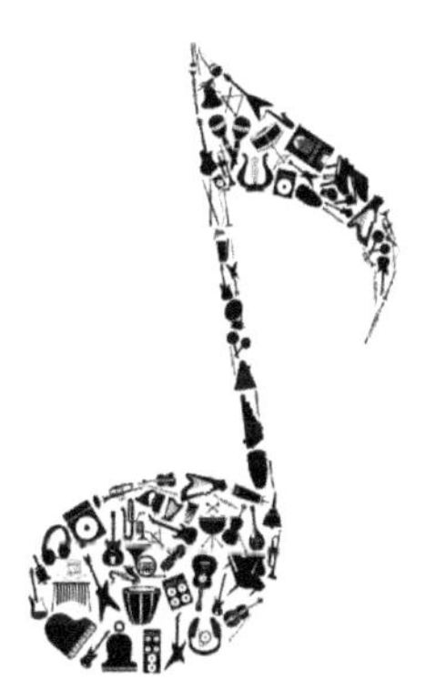

L'il Tootsie

At birth they are counted
To assure they are same
As an infant we all play
The piggies to market game

We walk, and stub them
Then yell our self hoarse
We coddle and clod them
As a matter of course

Some of us twirled
And flexed them en pointe
Taped, and then bandaged
The sore little joints

Now as an adult
Grab with them as hands
My favorite time
Is when they're buried in sand

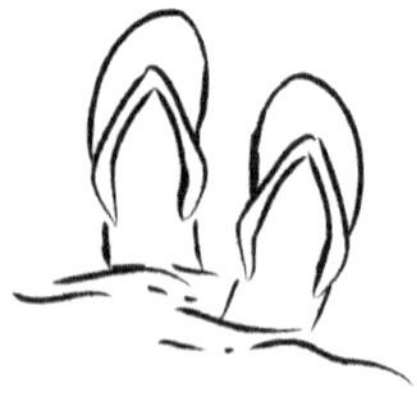

Midnight Dreaming

Twisted and turning
In blankets and throws
Some sweet like a flower
Or innocuous prose

Wake with a start
Or just to slack thirst
Continue the Dream,
What could be worse

Come soft as velvet
Slow as a drive
Can shatter your peace
Wake up and then cry

See your face in the night
Through that hazy mist
Forget the timbre
But remembered the Lizst

Some nights I just blink
To the dark I surrender
Others I wake
And play my heart's defender

Each morning I rise
And shake off my slumber
Do you ever dream of me?
I am oft left to wonder

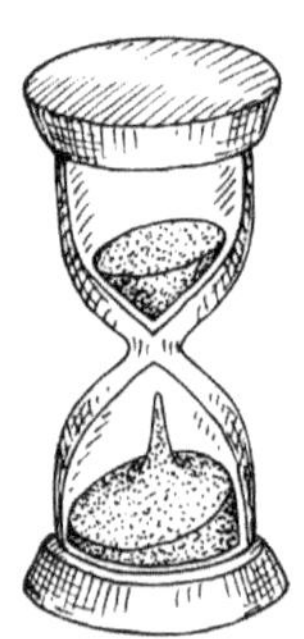

30

Long Weekend

Pack up the car and hit the highways
Adventure abounds, or so I'm told
Anticipation of what's to come
Out here, I'm of queen of the road

Playlist on blast, singing my tunes
Til my heart's so full it near bursts
Head off the exit, stop for some gas,
and see the road stops less traversed

I love that feeling of getting there
Almost like falling in love
No way to tell what's yet to come
Top down, blue skies up above

Passing the traffic on both sides
I have no worries or rules
Just ambling down to my destination
My ledfoot habit consumes

Road trip is over, my visit is done
Time to pack up again
I love the feeling on my way home
The ending is yet a time to begin.

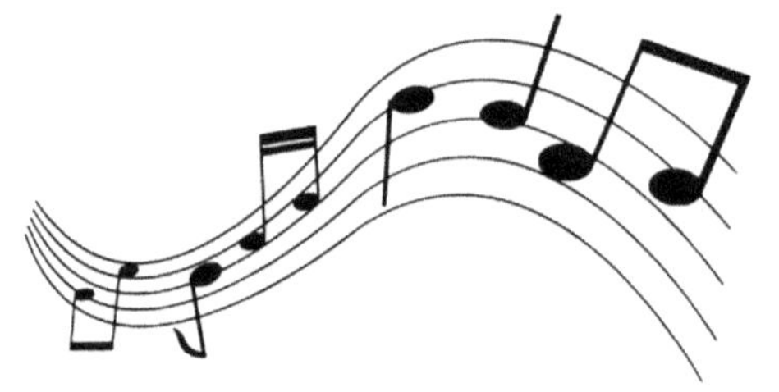

Save

Save me a spot
Save the memory
Save the date
Save me a plate
Save the last dance for me
Save face
Save dignity
Save me some time
Save wisdom
Save us from unfair persecution
Save me from myself
Save a life
Save all the things we left behind

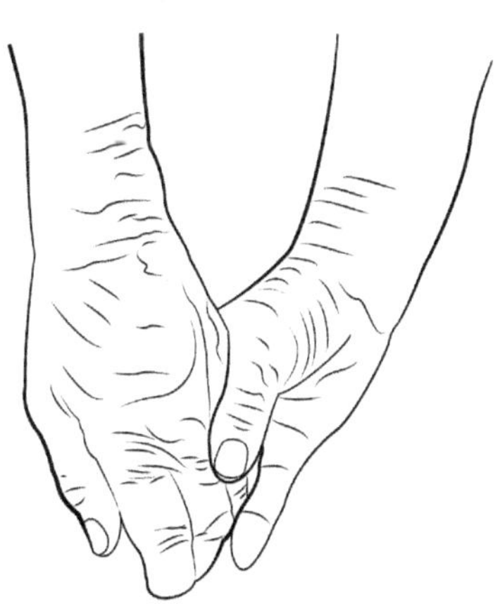

(maybe) She'll Never Know

…How she looks through another's eyes
(A lesson in perception, never learned)
…What it is to not offer kindness first
(Oblivious of others intentions)
…Patience is her virtue
(Merely stubborn or just plain incorrigible)
…How to utter goodbye
(An adept artist at the Irish sort)
…What the spotlight feels like
(Preferring to relay the message instead)
…How she has impacted others
(Refusing any compliment or thanks)
…What material wealth is
(Lives her life purely by simple means)
…The ugliness of the world
(Seeing light and love in everything)
…What it means to put herself first
(Attending to others is what she does best)
…Where the Bird and Fish would live if they
fell in love
(What if and If only can break your heart)
…If she is Someone he has met before
(What's meant for you, you never miss)
…For certain if anything at all was meant by it
(Stays Tangled Up In Blue)

…How to hang her head in despair
(Smiles proudly, not perfectly, at all the beauty
life has given)

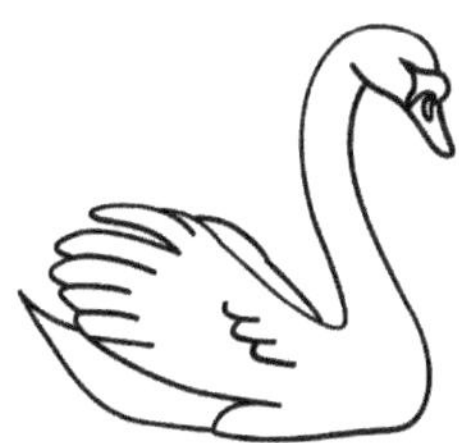

Promise of Hope

They come to us new,
Smelling so sweet.
If we're lucky,
Not a mark.
From their scalp
To their feet.

Old souls
With journeys
Under their belts.
Fresh bodies
With no words
Crying for help.

Swaddled
And cuddled
Just as they should be.
It's not true
you can spoil them,
You're their acting trustee.

We keep safe
And secure.
We teach them our ways.
If we're lucky

They visit
On important days

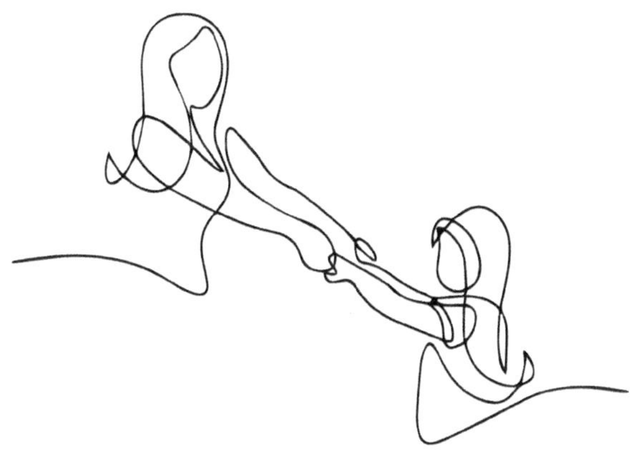